GLASS ENGRAVING FOR FUN AND PROFIT!

By Robert H. Scott, Jr.

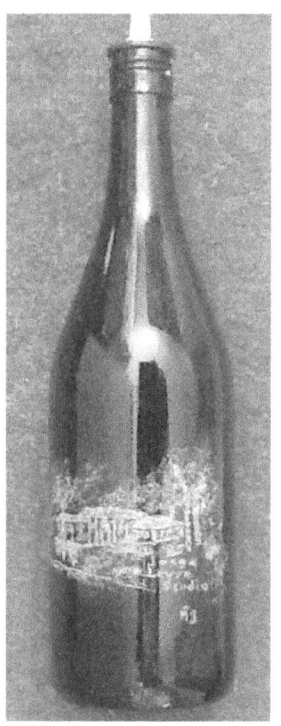

Copyright 2013, All Rights Reserved

Table of Contents

Introduction	3
Chapter 1 Examples of engraved glass by the author	8
Chapter 2 The tools needed to engrave on glass	8
Chapter 3. Safety tips before we begin	9
Chapter 4. The glass, where to get it and what works best	10
Chapter 5. The subjects to engrave	11
Chapter 6. Freehand or other techniques	12
Chapter 7. Getting started	13
Chapter 8. Problems and their solution	15
Chapter 9. Glass engraving as a business	16
Resources and Links	17
Notes	19

INTRODUCTION

Engraving on glass started by accident for the author. I bought an engraving tool to engrave a medical alert bracelet for my late wife. Unfortunately it did not work for that purpose. But later I wondered if it could be used to engrave on a small wine carafe. I started by drawing on the glass an outline but quickly found that this was an unnecessary step and now I do all the work freehand.

The tools you need to do engraving on glass are simple and available either locally or on Amazon.com with minimal expense. You need spend no more than $50 and probably less to get started. References will be provided at the end of this book to the items that I use in my work.

For safety if you do not wear glasses you will need light weight goggles to be sure no glass debris gets in your eyes. You will also need a mask to avoid breathing in any of the glass dust. And you will want to use a wet paper towel perhaps to clean up your work area so glass dust does not get blown around the area when you finish your work for the day.

You can do this as a fun hobby or it can also be a profit making enterprise. For the author it is a rewarding hobby and source of gifts for family and friends. But if you are interested in the business potential several ideas will be presented in the book for your consideration.

If you decide to try this I wish you good luck and hope that this book will be helpful in getting started and in sharing what I have learned over several years of working in this media. Hopefully it will give you pleasure and perhaps profit.

CHAPTER 1. EXAMPLES OF GLASS ENGRAVING BY THE AUTHOR

Glass is everywhere and you will find all sorts of opportunities to find glass media for engraving once you begin to think about it.

I started with a simple vase, also serving as a wine carafe.   This was done by using a marker and outlining the image of grapes on the vine on the glass and then engraving over the image. I quickly found that freehand without first making a drawing worked best for me. You may find this works for you.   However, on clear glass you can also size an image on your computer and tape it to the inside of the glass and do your engraving from this image. Obviously this does not work well with a wine bottle (good luck getting that inside!) or any dark glass.   Below are other carafes and a wine bottle. All were done freehand.

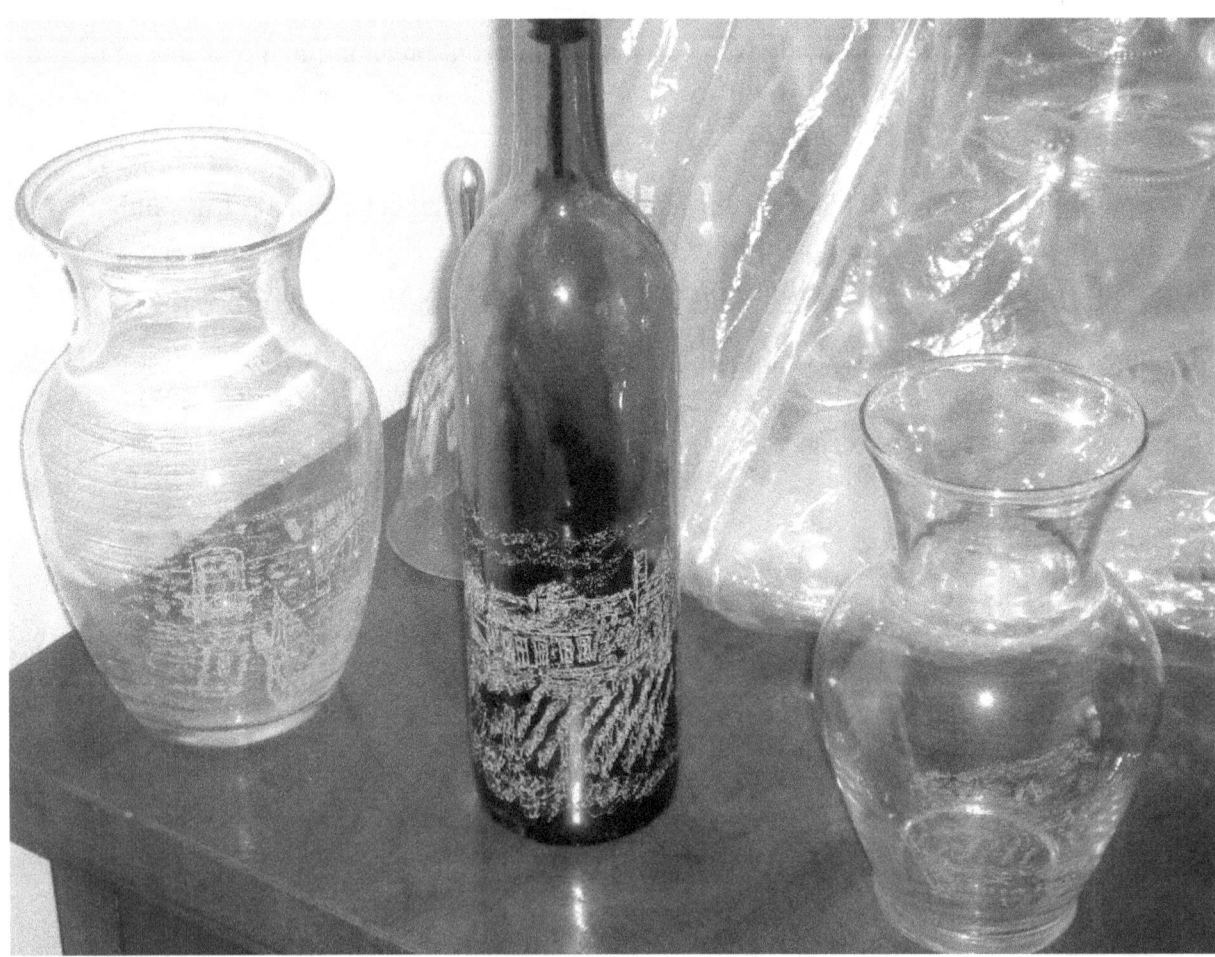

Darker glass is better for showing your design. Below are several wine bottles showing various shades of glass. The first one is in very light glass and to show this off coffee has been funneled into the bottle. You could also use cold coffee or dark wine or even sand to show off the bottle engraving. Note how the darker bottles show off the designs better than light bottles.

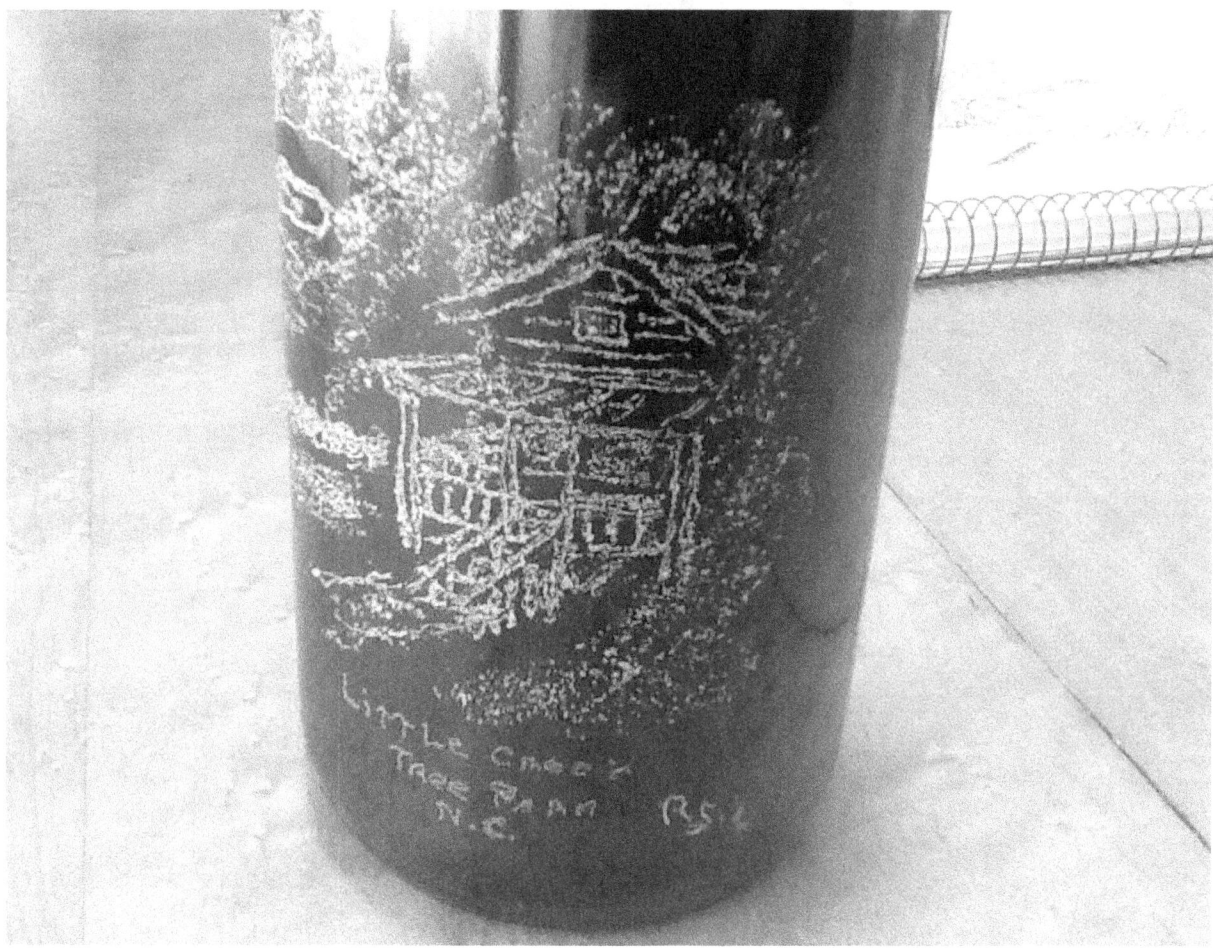

I keep olive oil and also an oil and vinegar mix in some of my bottles and while these do not show off the engraving well they are useful.

An example of how you can use this media for gifts is a bottle recently done showing the design of an artist's studio building.

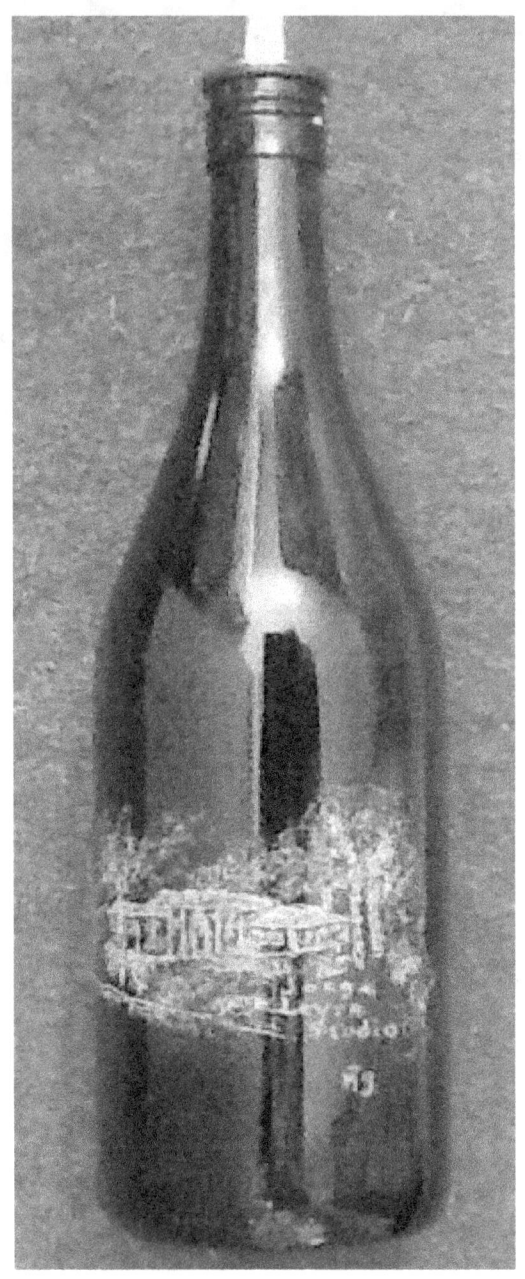

Finally, I have recently started working on canisters which have four flat sides. This gives me more than one surface to engrave. I use one of these for storing coffee which sets off the design nicely. Again, you could buy a small bag of play sand and fill this with sand if you like. And you do not have to engrave all four sides although this does seem to work well as the example below illustrates.

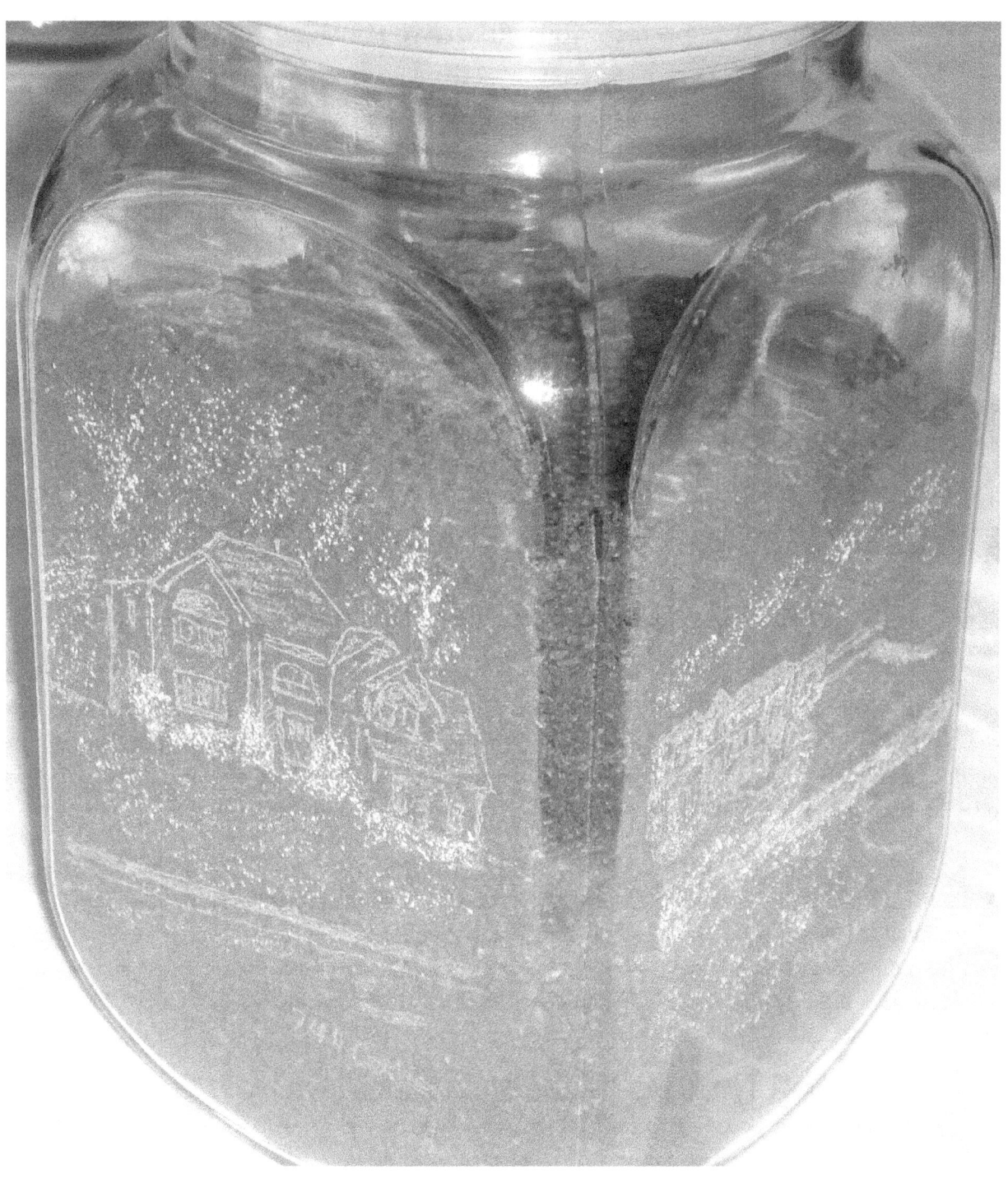

CHAPTER 2. THE TOOLS YOU WILL NEED TO ENGRAVE ON GLASS

Engraving on glass can be very inexpensive for you, or you can buy more sophisticated equipment at higher cost if that turns out to work for you. At the back of this book are some resources for you to consider both for other books on glass engraving and links to the basic tools that I use. The books mentioned also have places for acquiring supplies.

I suggest you start small, both in terms of equipment and cost. A Dremel engraving tool is inexpensive on Amazon and you may find this is all you need. A link to this tool is included at the back of this book along with other tools and items mentioned below. You will likely need an extension cord unless your work area is immediately adjacent to an outlet. This Dremel is not the same as the rotary Dremel but is a vibrating engraving tool.

I have bought diamond bits for the Dremel but frankly most of the time I only use the steel bit that came with the Dremel. You will need a small but sturdy screwdriver to occasionally tighten the bits or to put in different bits.

Either glasses or a pair of inexpensive goggles which you can find at any hardware store along with a dust mask will be needed. These will be discussed more in Chapter 3.

A tool that I have used that is helpful is a small pen size battery operated rotary engraver. It differs from the Dremel in that it rotates rather than vibrates. It can be used for fine work or signatures and for this purpose works extremely well. This will be listed in the resource list at the end of the book. I have purchased added bits for this engraving tool as well but have not used them as the bit that came with the tool works has been all I have needed so far.

Additional bits are not expensive, at least not on Amazon. If you are an Amazon Prime member you can often get all of this with no shipping cost. If not a Prime member you can take a temporary membership and cancel in the first month owing nothing and still get two day delivery and free shipping. I have found Amazon a good source of this equipment but you can also find this at local hobby or hardware stores.

Other items you will need will be a work space with good lighting. This can be a kitchen table or other small table as you do not need much space. The area should be well lit. You will need to clean up any glass dust that develops and I use a wet paper towel for this purpose.

If you are not comfortable working free hand you may want to use mostly clear glass and sources of this will be mentioned later. If this is glass that you can reach inside, like a vase or canister, you can use tape and put a picture inside the glass and use this as your template for starting your engraving.

I keep a small gym type bag in which I keep books, tools, extension cord for the drill, extra batteries and pictures that I may want to work from doing engraving

CHAPTER 3. SAFETY TIPS BEFORE WE BEGIN

I have already mentioned the basic safety items. Glasses or goggles and a dust mask. Goggles need not be safety type but merely enough to keep any glass particles from the engraving getting in your eyes. I use my regular glasses.

There are several types of dust mask. The better ones I find obstruct my glasses and so I generally use the ones you can find at any drug store inexpensively. They can be used more than one time as their purpose is to keep you from breathing any glass dust. If someone is sitting with you while you are working you need to be sure they are also protected.

If you have children or pets around your work area you need to be observant to be sure they too are protected, or best of all kept away from your work area. Working deeper inside a desk or table will keep any small particles near the work you are doing.

When you finish a project, either for the day or several hours, you need to sweep up the glass particles and I find that a wet paper towel works well to pick up any small pieces. There will not be much and it is more like glass dust. All the more reason to use your safety equipment! You do not want to breath in this dust.

It is handy to keep a slightly wet paper towel on your work area along with a dry towel to wipe off the work as you proceed to see better how it is looking and to clean off small glass particles. Once wet the design will tend to disappear so you use the dry towel to make the image visible faster.

If you are using the Dremel or other plugged in tool always be sure to unplug it after use, especially if you have young (or even older) children around who might be tempted to turn it on and use it.

One last safety tip and this is more for safety of your work than your personal safety. It is better to use softer glass than harder. Leaded crystal is obviously the softest glass but also the most expensive. You will probably find that vases and wine bottles are softer than canisters. Only by trial and error will you know what works best for you. On harder glass the rotary pen type of tool seems to work best for early work. Be sure to use glass that is thicker than thinner. Thin glass can break which will not only ruin your work but if it shatters can cause injury. Also, when running the Dremel engraver be sure to have it set on the lowest possible speed. I made the mistake early on of using higher speeds and cracked one vase. I was able to save the work by drawing over the small crack but it was annoying and I learned my lesson! Fortunately it was an inexpensive glass vase.

CHAPTER 4. THE GLASS, WHERE TO GET IT AND WHAT WORKS BEST

Starting with the cheapest first! Have friends save you any wine bottles they may have that will work for you. The darker the glass the better. The biggest problem you will have is removing the labels. There are some label removing systems but I find that soaking them in hot water and then steaming them either with a steamer or a kettle and scraping off the labels with a dull knife works best. It is a bit of a chore but it is not that bad once you get the hang of it. Unfortunately there will be gunk left on the bottle. To remove that you will need a product like "Goo Gone" that I buy at Home Depot. I use paper towels with the Goo Gone and then wash and dry the bottles. I do several at one time so they will be ready when I want to do engraving.

If you are good at freehand work and do not need to trace a design then dark glass or dark wine bottles will work the best. Lighter or clear bottles or glass will work but you will need something to show off the design such as colored paper , dark wine, coffee, sand or any number of other items you might find that work to let the engraving stand out .

Softer glass is better than harder glass. Wine bottles vary in hardness as do vases. Canisters I find tend to be very hard glass. One inexpensive source of these is either Disabled American Veterans stores or Goodwill or Salvation Army. Another source is garage sales and flea markets. Or Michaels or Hobby Lobby. Hobby Lobby weekly (Sunday) and on their website have 40% off on regular price merchandise one item a day. So if you are buying canisters you can use that to reduce the cost. They have a nice selection of clear glass items that will work well for you.

If you or friends have flowers delivered in vases be sure to save (or have friends save for you) these glass vases as they will work very well for engraving.

As mentioned earlier, leaded crystal is probably the softest glass but finding that can be tricky. Buying retail is expensive so best to check out the inexpensive sources such as flea markets and garage sales. Take with you on these trips a stainless steel spoon or knife. Why? Because if you lightly tap the glass with the spoon or knife leaded glass will ring like a bell compared to a very dull and flat sound from non leaded glass. This is not 100% guaranteed to find you leaded glass but it is an inexpensive way to do a quick test. If you have some glass around the house that you know is leaded and other than you know is not test it at home and learn the difference in the sound. The more lead in the glass by the way the more it will "ring" when tapped.

CHAPTER 5. THE SUBJECTS TO ENGRAVE

Obviously the subjects you choose will be ones you find you can engrave well and ones which you find aesthetically pleasing. If you are doing this as a business you want designs that will sell! You may want local scenes, seasonal scenes such as Christmas designs.

You do not want to choose extensively elaborate designs to start with but you do not have to limit yourself to very simple designs either. I started with a bunch of grapes on a vine. Then I moved quickly to scenes of Venice, Provence and Tuscany showing Provence and Tuscan villas with grape vines. Those images went well with the wine bottle used as olive oil pourer and storage bottle.

Keep a file of any pictures you run across that you think will make a pleasing engraving. If adept on the computer you will find any number of images you can print out and use. If you are not comfortable doing your work freehand then you will want to size pictures so you can trim them to fit inside the vase, canister or other item you plan to engrave. Then you can tape this inside the clear glass and use as a template for engraving. I have not done this very often but you may find it will help you to start.

Any artist will find they do some things well and others less well. Obviously you want to choose subjects that you feel comfortable drawing and which will be pleasing as a completed work.

It is best to experiment with inexpensive glass to start until you get the feel of how best to express subjects in this media. Some subjects work better than others. The engraving process I use does not work with extremely fine detail. I have never tried a portrait for example. Scenes as those shown in examples above work for me and may for you.

Depending on the subject, you may want to draw some rough outlines or corner markers on the glass with your tool before you begin and if you are working freehand this is recommended. The peak of houses for example or a line where the foreground stops for a road. And as you progress you will want to wipe the area clean and this will often show areas needing work. For this reason scenes seem to work best for me and I avoid anything that requires fine detail. The vibrating Dremel or the rotating pen tool are not designed for extremely fine work. This is not etching of glass but engraving. There is a big difference and the subject and techniques are entirely different, as you will quickly see once you begin working on glass.

CHAPTER 6. FREEHAND OR OTHER TECHNIQUES

As mentioned above I started by using a glass marker and drawing a design on my first vase. I quickly found that this was both awkward and hard to see the work as I progressed. So my next effort was one done freehand and for me this worked. But this will depend on your skill as an artist. Some are very good at freehand drawing and if that is you this will be your best technique.

To start you may want to place small marks at various places on the surface to guide you as you draw on the glass. You can then begin to fill in detail later. This will help to keep your proportions and make filling in much easier. At this point I simply start and do not use this technique except on rare occasion but it is likely best you begin this way until you become comfortable with the media and tools.

A technique mentioned above is to use a magic marker designed to mark on glass and to draw your design either in detail or outline on the glass. You can also (except on bottles of course) use tape and affix a copy of the item you are engraving inside the glass surface and then either use your magic marker to affix a design or outline or work directly on the glass with the design inside. Be sure to use enough tape so that when the vibration starts it does not loosen the tape inside taking away your template or allowing it to slip. It is a good idea to put marks outside on the corners of the template just in case it slips. That way you can easily tape it back where it was and continue working. If you are working on a vase or other glass item where the surface is not flat you may want to stuff it with a cotton dish towel to press the image against the glass. You may even need to do this with a flat surface.

On curved surfaces you will find that it is often hard to draw straight lines horizontally. You can use a straight edge to help and the author often finds that turning the glass sideways or at an angle helps. If the line is not straight often you can go over it several times to straighten it. Making it thicker sometimes helps too.

On harder glass you may find that you have to press harder with the tool and on hard glass I tend to work first with the pen rotary tool and then go back for rougher work or to thicken designs with the Dremel. You are likely to find that curved or flat surfaces need different techniques and different pressures. Experimenting will quickly tell you what works best for you. Each artist will develop their own unique technique in this media and you should find those tools and surfaces and designs that fit your talent and personality.

As for signatures or lettering you are likely to find the pen rotary tool the best. Again you can freehand the letters or you can adhere them printed from computer or otherwise to the surface and engrave over them. Even on a bottle you can paste lettering to the bottle and engrave through the paper and when the paper is removed you can then go over the lettering to darken and improve. At this point you may even find the Dremel vibrating tool will work as well or better. Again, let experience guide you and try different tools and techniques until you are comfortable finding what works best for you.

CHAPTER 7. GETTING STARTED

The first step is to set up your work space. I use my kitchen table and my typical set up is shown below. You can use a card table or any surface with good lighting and sufficient space. A dark surface is good as it will help you to see the engraving as you progress. Of course you will need an outlet in which to plug the Dremel if you are using this tool and will probably need an extension cord. I use a small bag (shown) to store my equipment when not working with it and you may want to do something similar.

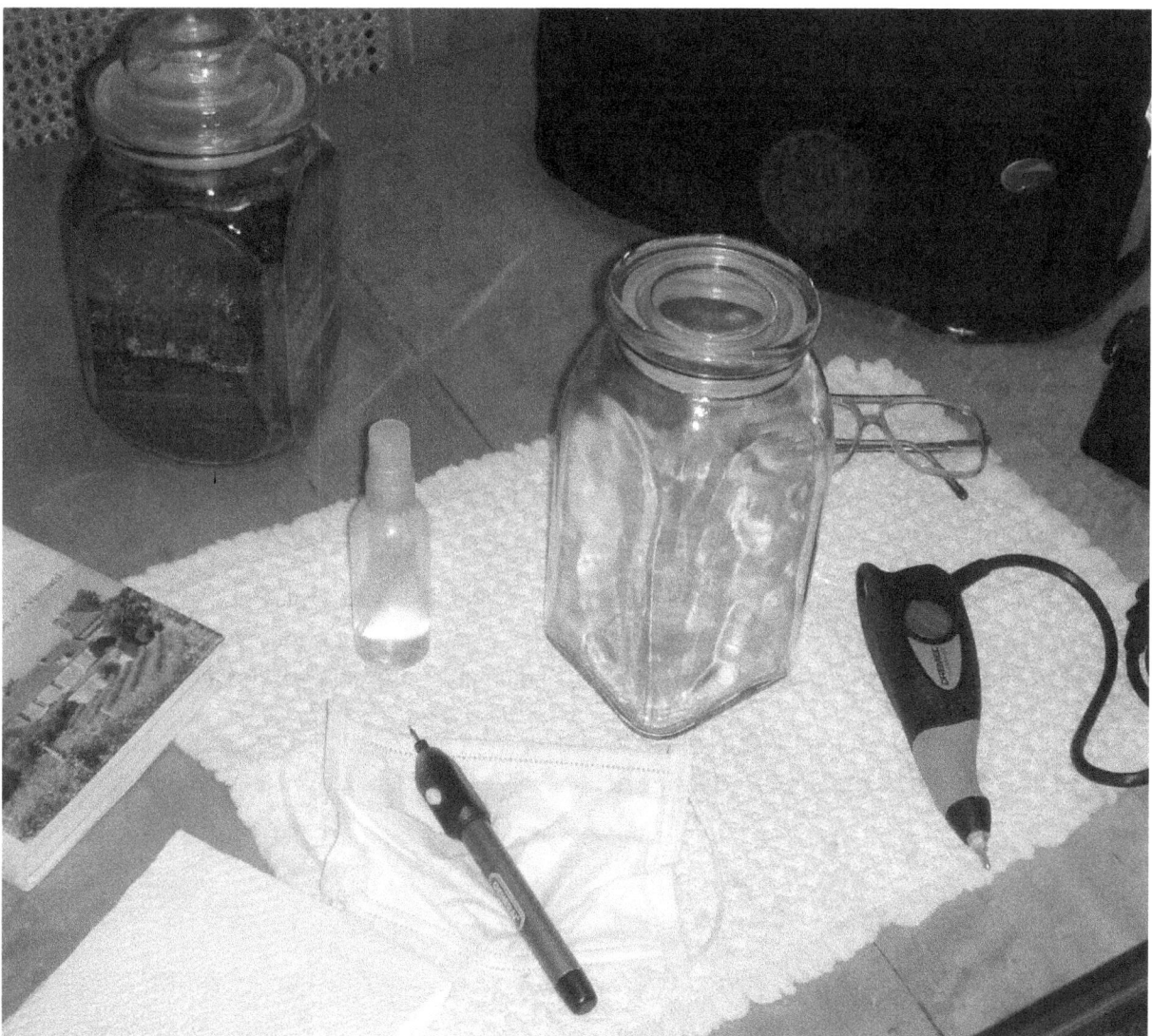

Once the work area is set up you will want some paper towels or cotton towels and some water that you will use both to clean up at the end and to occasionally wipe the surface on which you are working so you can see your design clearly. I prefer paper towels so I can dispose of them easily when done. I use a small spray bottle filled with water. You may also need something dark (a cloth, paper, etc.) to put inside any clear glass you are working on so you can see your work more clearly. The dark wood of my kitchen table works for me. Of course if you are working from a design taped inside this will not be needed until you remove that picture and begin to complete your work.

If you are working on a wine bottle, which is my suggestion for starting to learn to do this work, you will not have a design inside to work from. If you are comfortable working freehand it is best that you use the Dremel or the pen rotary tool to place marks visible to you at various key points along the design. Then start with straight lines which you may find difficult at first. You will need to practice to learn to do this right. Don't get discouraged if your first effort shows crooked wavy lines that should be straight. It will take practice to draw straight lines in this media. Also you may find you are timid at the start and do not press down hard enough to make a mark. You will get over this quickly once you keep working at the technique. But do not press too hard, especially on thin glass (which is not recommended for this work), and be sure on the Dremel you have the setting at the lowest speed and vibration. If you are working on a wine bottle this will not be much of a problem but on a vase you can find you will crack the vase. If this happens you may be able to freehand a design along the crack to disguise the mistake.

Once you have the basic outline in place you will wipe the design and see what areas need work. You will likely want to lightly fill wall areas and you can use the Dremel to make good cloud effects or grass areas as shown in some of the examples above. A lot of this you will have to learn by doing until you find what works best for you. Your artistic sensibilities will guide you and after a while working with glass engraving you will find your own special effects.

Once you finish your design you can go over it with gold or silver finish if this appeals to you. I have done this but find for my taste a clear design is the most appealing. You can buy leafing at most hobby stores either in sheets or bottles to use on your designs.

If you are working with wine bottles you will probably want to finish with either corks or a pourer which you can get at hobby stores or stores like Bed, Bath and Beyond or off Amazon. You may find that the pourer is the most expensive part of your project! So finding these inexpensively is worth the hunt.

Once you have finished your work you will want to wash off the area to get all the glass bits removed and then dry to look over the work and be sure nothing more is needed to complete your work.

CHAPTER 8. PROBLEMS AND THEIR SOLUTION

You will encounter problems rather quickly. Learning how to handle the Dremel or the pen rotary tool will take practice. Lines will wobble early on and even later in the process. But if you do not give up you will find you can go over even a wobbly line and make it straighter if not perfectly straight. One thing not to expect in engraving on glass with the techniques is this book is very fine detailed work as in etching glass. At least I have not found this possible.

Small cracks in glass can often be disguised by going over them with the engraving tool lightly and incorporating them into the design. This has happened only once to me and that was on a vase I was working on using higher speeds on the Dremel as I was experimenting learning to do this work.. Since then it has not happened and hopefully will not in your projects.

Be sure to keep a screwdriver handy in case the bit becomes loose when working and falls out. That happens occasionally and so I always keep a screwdriver handy.

You may want to keep a small flashlight handy too in case you need to see some detail that your other lighting will not show up. A magnifying glass may be helpful too. And you will want to wipe clean with a wet towel the work area and then dry it to see what areas need work.

Many of the techniques will only be learned by doing. A book can help you to get started but you will have to learn how to handle the tools to get the best effects that satisfy your artistic sensibilities. Often you will find a wavy line can either be modified to work or worked over to achieve a different effect.

One problem to note if you are working on wine bottles. You will find there is a seam on most of these running the length of the bottle on each side. You want to do your work between those seams so be sure to turn the bottle so the seam is to the side and not running into your design. Yes, I have made that mistake!

Working in clear glass it is often hard to see your design. A flashlight may help and putting a colored towel inside will also help or you can use colored tissue paper. Anything dark that will let your design stand out. If your work area is dark that will work well. If you are putting a picture inside as a template you may want to lightly wet that paper so it will stick to the inside of the glass and mold to the glass especially curved glass. Then you can tape the picture to the glass.

Displaying your work will again require some creative thinking. I have used colored tissue paper to good effect as well as special lighting. In a canister or even a light colored or clear bottle you can use dark coffee as a filler and that makes the design stand out. Examples are shown earlier in the book. Sand can be used in bottles used only for show and same is true of vases. Dark sand can be found although any sand is likely to work. Any dark liquid will also set off a design. One advantage to sand is that it will make the object heavy and therefore less likely to be accidentally overturned. If you have small children or clumsy friends this can be an advantage.

CHAPTER 9. GLASS ENGRAVING AS A BUSINESS

I am probably not the best source for information on this subject as I do my engraving only as a hobby for personal use and as gifts for family and friends. However, I have been approached numerous times suggesting I sell some of my engraving. So here are a few thoughts to consider if you are an artist interested in making a profit from your engraving.

You may consider approaching local realtors suggesting that you engrave on a wine bottle or canister of their choice scenes of a house they have sold so they can give the end product as a house warming gift. In Cincinnati, Ohio where I lived for many years realtors gave framed watercolor pictures of houses they sold and it was a welcome gift and one you could take to your next home to remember the last one. I have two of these in my own home from days in Cincinnati. The same could be true of a wine bottle on which a house is engraved. Used for olive oil with a pourer this can be a nice but relatively inexpensive gift. I would likely require only an hour from start to finish to do a bottle of this sort but you would need to see how long it would take you and price your work accordingly.

I have done scenes of businesses for friends one of whom is an artist and the cover photo is the scene done of his studio. Another was a dentist that lost his office in a tornado and the scene was a gift with an engraving showing his new office.

Another source of commissions is to do scenes of someone's boat or pet or their vacation home or any other image they might want engraved. The author did one for his son of his university on the Jersey shore on one side of a canister, his home on another, their beach club area and finally an access from back of his home to an adjoining park. That is the canister shown earlier.

Scenes of vineyards and Provence or Tuscan villas make for excellent subjects for gift items which could be commissioned or sold in gift shops. As with any business what sells is what works and you may have to find by trial and error what works best for you. If you are doing wine bottles for use with olive oil or other liquids you can use corks or pourers. Corks are cheaper but less useful. But depending on price corks may be just fine. The buyer can find a pourer they like if that is the use they want to make of it.

Obviously seasonal items such as Christmas or Easter scenes may appeal. Or some local scene that is familiar to prospective buyers of your engraved glass.

I have been approached to do engraving for birthdays but any event such as weddings, anniversaries, or retirement can be a source of business for an artist working in engraving glass.

You are likely to have fifty other ideas but hopefully these will help you get a start if it is your desire to do engraving for profit. But whether for profit or for pleasure it is hoped you find this a fun and enjoyable way to express your artistic expression.

RESOURCES AND LINKS

I bought most of my tools off Amazon.com using my Prime Membership for free shipping and quick delivery.

The main tool is the Dremel engraving tool and you can either word search for "engraving tool" or use the following link. But as with all the links these can change so if this does not bring up the item be sure to do a search under engraving tools. A link is also included for diamond bits and for the rotary pen tool discussed above. **If you order bits be sure you order the correct size of bit**. The Dremel usually takes a $1/8^{th}$ shank while the rotary pen tool uses a $1/32^{nd}$ shank. And check for the lowest price as well.

Dremel engraving tool link: http://www.amazon.com/Dremel-290-01-Stroke-Engraver-Template/dp/B0000302YN/ref=sr_1_2?ie=UTF8&qid=1383836064&sr=8-2&keywords=engraving+tools

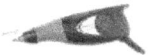

Rotary pen engraving tool link: http://www.amazon.com/General-Tools-505-Cordless-Precision/dp/B004YK66NM/ref=sr_1_1?ie=UTF8&qid=1383836064&sr=8-1&keywords=engraving+tools

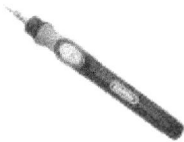

Dremel bit set link: http://www.amazon.com/20pc-Diamond-Grinding-Burr-Shank/dp/B008UZ1A2Y/ref=pd_sim_hi_7

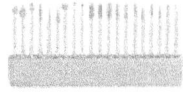

Rotary pen bit set link: http://www.amazon.com/20pc-Diamond-Grinding-Burr-Shank/dp/B008UZ1A2Y/ref=pd_sim_hi_1

A couple of books on glass engraving are included below. Others can be found by searching for "Engraving on Glass" under books on Amazon.com

http://www.amazon.com/Engraving-Glass-Beginners-Boyd-Graham/dp/0486266834/ref=sr_1_1?s=books&ie=UTF8&qid=1383836608&sr=1-1&keywords=glass+engraving

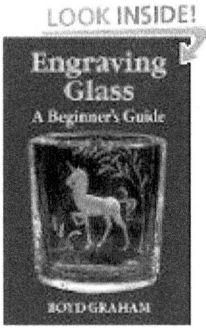

http://www.amazon.com/Glass-Engraving-Techniques-Stuart-Palmer/dp/0713460083/ref=sr_1_7?s=books&ie=UTF8&qid=1383836613&sr=1-7&keywords=glass+engraving

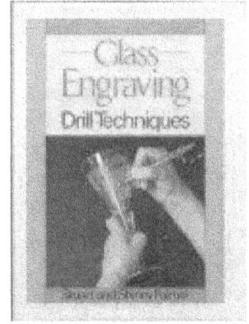

Notes on Your Engraving

Date

Type of Glass

Hardness of Glass

Subject

Time to Complete

Results

If Sold Sales Outlet

If Sold Sales Made

Notes on Your Engraving

Date

Type of Glass

Hardness of Glass

Subject

Time to Complete

Results

If Sold Sales Outlet

If Sold Sales Made

Notes on Your Engraving

Date

Type of Glass

Hardness of Glass

Subject

Time to Complete

Results

If Sold Sales Outlet

If Sold Sales Made

Notes on Your Engraving

Date

Type of Glass

Hardness of Glass

Subject

Time to Complete

Results

If Sold Sales Outlet

If Sold Sales Made

Notes on Your Engraving

Date

Type of Glass

Hardness of Glass

Subject

Time to Complete

Results

If Sold Sales Outlet

If Sold Sales Made

Notes on Your Engraving

Date

Type of Glass

Hardness of Glass

Subject

Time to Complete

Results

If Sold Sales Outlet

If Sold Sales Made

Notes on Your Engraving

Date

Type of Glass

Hardness of Glass

Subject

Time to Complete

Results

If Sold Sales Outlet

If Sold Sales Made

Notes on Your Engraving

Date

Type of Glass

Hardness of Glass

Subject

Time to Complete

Results

If Sold Sales Outlet

If Sold Sales Made

Notes on Your Engraving

Date

Type of Glass

Hardness of Glass

Subject

Time to Complete

Results

If Sold Sales Outlet

If Sold Sales Made

Notes on Your Engraving

Date

Type of Glass

Hardness of Glass

Subject

Time to Complete

Results

If Sold Sales Outlet

If Sold Sales Made

Notes on Your Engraving

Date

Type of Glass

Hardness of Glass

Subject

Time to Complete

Results

If Sold Sales Outlet

If Sold Sales Made